IMAGES
*of America*

# OCEAN CITY'S
# HISTORIC HOTELS

# OCEAN CITY, N.J.

Showing its Unrivalled Location, Beautiful Sea-Shore, Protected Sailing Waters and Famous Fishing Grounds, also Railroad and Ferry Connections.
Artesian Water, Sanitary Sewage, Electric Lights, Gas, Electric Cars.

In this 1903 map of Ocean City, the campground, between Fifth and Sixth Streets and Wesley and Asbury Avenues, is in the center. Most of the early hotels and guesthouses were located between Fourth and Eleventh Streets, close to the campground, the train stations, and the ferry wharf. This map touts the city's attractions, including "Unrivalled Location, Beautiful Seashore, Protected Sailing Waters and Famous Fishing Grounds." (Authors' collection.)

ON THE COVER: The Ocean City Beach Patrol took a group photograph at the end of each summer to commemorate another successful year of saving lives and preventing injuries to bathers. The photograph was always taken on the beach near the patrol's headquarters, with the Flanders Hotel in the background. This photograph is of the 1925 lifeguard squad. (Authors' collection.)

IMAGES
*of America*

# OCEAN CITY'S
# HISTORIC HOTELS

Fred and Susan Miller

ARCADIA
PUBLISHING

Published by Arcadia Publishing
Charleston, South Carolina


Library of Congress Control Number: 2013955122

For all general information, please contact Arcadia Publishing:
Telephone 843-853-2070
Fax 843-853-0044
E-mail sales@arcadiapublishing.com
For customer service and orders:
Toll-Free 1-888-313-2665

Visit us on the Internet at www.arcadiapublishing.com

*This book is dedicated to Stu Sirott for 10 years of technical know-how and hard work—books, magazines, and newspapers.*

# CONTENTS

# ACKNOWLEDGMENTS

We would like to thank Stu Sirott for his technical knowledge and hard work. Without his help, this book would not exist. We would also like to thank Susan's sister and brother-in-law, Joan and Allan Okin, for their editing skills.

Barb and Dean Adams have graciously given us access to Barb's collection of hotel images, as has the Ocean City Historical Museum (OCHM). Kitty and Sal Paone, Carol and Bill Dotts, Rahn G. Brackin, and Jeanne Kirkman have also lent photographs. Unless otherwise noted, the images come from the authors' collection.

Many of the captions have quotations taken directly from brochures printed and given out by the hotel's management as advertisements.

# INTRODUCTION

It has been said that hotels helped build Ocean City into the successful community that it is today. Ocean City was founded in 1879 by five Methodist ministers—the Reverends William H. Burrell and William B. Wood and brothers S. Wesley Lake, Ezra B. Lake, and James E. Lake—and the Lake brothers' father, Simon Lake. Their aim was to build a Christian seaside resort, much like that of Ocean Grove, New Jersey, several miles to the north. But the men envisioned one big difference between Ocean City and Ocean Grove: theirs would be a year-round community as well as a summer retreat.

To that end, they quickly organized a government run by the Ocean City Association, brought their families to live here, started a school, printed a newspaper, and encouraged tradesmen and businessmen of all types to move to the fledgling city with their families. They recognized that transportation would be necessary to bring people from surrounding communities, so they built a railroad between Pleasantville and Somers Point, New Jersey, and bought a steamship to bring passengers across Great Egg Harbor Bay to Ocean City.

To introduce the new resort community, they organized excursions to bring people from as far away as Philadelphia, 60 miles to the west.

While building a community was uppermost, religion was never far from the minds of the founding members. They stipulated in all property deeds that there was to be no production or sale of alcoholic beverages, and they passed ordinances banning amusement and commercial activity on Sundays. During the summer, they organized religious retreats centered around a large tent on campgrounds between Wesley and Asbury Avenues and Fifth and Sixth Streets, where services and prayer meetings were held and different ministers spoke to the crowds. Visitors were able to bring their own tents to the campgrounds or rent tents for a small fee.

As the camp meetings grew in popularity and transportation to the island became easier, there was a great need to house the summer visitors. The first hotel, the Piqua, opened in 1880. Soon, more hotels and guesthouses were built. Many of the hotels stayed open throughout the year. By 1900, some 29 hotels had been built on the island. The seaside resort was a success!

But more than simple hotels were needed to keep the community flourishing. With the year-round population increasing, the school open, businesses of all kinds thriving, and a government working well, it was still felt by many residents that something was holding the city back from all that it could be. After much discussion and a study by a committee appointed by the chamber of commerce, it was decided that a new, large, modern, oceanfront hotel should be built. Such a structure was deemed necessary if the community was to keep up with its resort neighbors.

In 1922, the Ocean Front Hotel Corporation of Ocean City was organized, led by prominent local businessmen. It was charged with finding a location, constructing, and operating the new hotel. All city residents would have the opportunity to buy shares in the new corporation and thus participate in this endeavor. It was decided that the hotel would be built at Eleventh Street and the boardwalk. Ocean City native Vivian Smith was chosen as the architect. On July 28,

1923, the Flanders Hotel opened with much fanfare. Dignitaries from as far away as New York City attended the gala dinner, and newspapers from up and down the East Coast raved about the new hotel.

On October 11, 1927, the well-being created by the prosperity of these years was shattered by a devastating fire that started under the boardwalk at Ninth Street and spread west toward the central business district of the city. Many stores, businesses, and homes were destroyed before the blaze was brought under control. Flames could be seen in Somers Point across the bay, and fire companies from all over rushed to the city's aid. When the fire was finally halted, two of the largest and most opulent hotels, the Traymore and the Normandie-on-the-Sea, were gone. The Flanders Hotel, fortunately, had been spared.

As the city struggled to recover from the fire, it was found that nearly 500 hotel rooms had been destroyed. There was a great need for more rooms, but by late 1929, when the country was overtaken by the Great Depression, only a few new hotels had been built. The owners of those hotels made sure that they were advertised as "fireproof." World War II followed the Depression, and during the war, the federal government ordered all building be halted as the materials were needed for the war effort.

Although No Vacancy signs were commonplace in the summer after World War II, as the country slowly recovered, many families found themselves without the resources to spend their usual week or two at a hotel in Ocean City. Guesthouses were less-expensive alternatives that still allowed families to spend their vacations in their favorite seashore resort. Many of Ocean City's summer homes were very large houses, usually three stories, with numerous bedrooms and large living rooms. These were easily converted into guesthouses, which had the added attraction of making patrons truly feel like guests in the host's home. They offered a personal touch rarely found in a hotel.

Even though the hotels and guesthouses were doing well, there was concern about the future: modern motels were being built in neighboring resorts, giving the older hotels serious competition. In the spring of 1950, the local hotel and guesthouse owners, concerned that this would happen in Ocean City, convinced Mayor Edward Bowker and Commissioners Augustus S. Goetz and Henry Roeser Jr. to adopt an amendment to the zoning ordinance, forbidding the building of motels. Few new hotels were built during this time, possibly because developers were leery of building hotels at a time when motels seemed to be more desirable to the public. The ordinance was effective in keeping Ocean City motel-free until 1956, when a New Jersey Superior Court ruling stated that motels were legally permissible wherever hotels or guesthouses were allowed. A decade later, 14 motels had been built on the island.

Apartments also were a growing trend. They allowed families to have privacy and afforded guests the opportunity to save money by dining in. An apartment could often be rented for a month for the same price that one of the bigger hotels would cost for a week. They therefore became another popular alternative to hotel stays.

Guesthouses and summer rental apartments continued to flourish as the desirability of the older hotels began to wane. After the mid-1950s, those hotels located nearest the beach, those with dining rooms—especially if they also served meals to the public—or with other sought-after amenities, thrived. Some of the other hotels saw a loss of their clientele and, not too many years later, closed their doors.

# One

# THE HOTELS THAT BUILT OCEAN CITY

Supplying lodging and food for its visitors has been the major business of Ocean City from its earliest days. Parker Miller, the first inhabitant of the island, offered room and shelter to the group of men who came to survey the land, construct the streets, and cut brush for the new town. The first project of the city's developers was to erect a rooming house for the men who came to build the city's structures. Called Pioneer Cottage, the rooming house was on Asbury Avenue near Seventh Street.

By 1883, only four years after its 1879 founding, Ocean City was a growing resort with six hotels already built on the island. The Piqua, a small hotel across from the campgrounds, was the first. Large hotels included the Brighton Hotel, which opened in 1880 as the Ocean Hotel; the Wesley House (1881), and the Illinois House (1883). The Lake Cottage and the Atlantic Cottage, two small hotels, could accommodate several guests each. An early listing of hotels includes Aldine Cottage at Ninth Street and West Avenue, Coxes Cottage at Seventh Street and Asbury Avenue, Holly Grove Cottage at Central Avenue between Fourth and Fifth Streets, Haven House at Sixth Street and Ocean Avenue, and Minetola Cottage on Fourth Street near Asbury Avenue. No other information is available about them, and it is not known how long they existed.

Another guesthouse and 15 more hotels had been built on the island by 1895. Rooms at one of the large hotels, such as the Emmett at Eighth Street and Central Avenue, the Lafayette at Thirteenth Street and Central Avenue, or the Hewlings at Ninth Street and Wesley Avenue, could be had for $15 per week. A room, with meals included, could be rented at the smaller hotels for between 75¢ and $2 per day. Hotel guests returned year after year, and it was clear that Ocean City was quickly becoming one of the most successful summer resorts on the southern New Jersey shore.

The Parker Miller House, one of the first buildings on the island, accommodated the many sportsmen who came to Peck's Beach (the original name of the island) to hunt and fish. The house later hosted the men who came to survey the new city and construct its streets and houses. By 1882, Miller had opened his home as a guesthouse, which he called Atlantic Cottage. It had eight rooms and could accommodate 12 guests. In the early 1930s, the house, which had been at 726 Asbury Avenue, was moved to city ground in the hope of saving and restoring it. In 1939, however, it was deemed too badly deteriorated and was razed.

In 1871, the federal government built three Life-Saving Service stations on the island—one at either end, and one in the middle. They were manned during the winter months, when most shipwrecks occurred, by a keeper and a crew of seven men. It was their responsibility to look for ships in distress, rescue the sailors, and offer them shelter in the station. The one shown here was at the southern end of the island.

Founded as a Christian seaside resort, Ocean City held religious services in a large tent on the campground, a square bounded by Fifth Street, Wesley Avenue, Sixth Street, and Asbury Avenue. Those who came to the camp meetings could put up tents of their own or rent tents for use on the campgrounds. The tents came in different sizes and could be rented for different periods of time. The rates went from $1 per week for a nine-by-nine-foot tent, to $5.25 per week for a tent 14 feet by 21 feet.

In 1921, the name of the Hotel Piqua was changed to the Park View Hotel. The three-story building, with a mansard-style roof and dormer windows, is in the Second Empire style.

When Jean Blundin Campbell bought the Park View in 1938, she changed the name to the Parkside Hotel. Campbell also owned the Chatterbox Restaurant, at Ninth Street and Central Avenue. Her parents, Elizabeth and William Blundin, had owned the Biscayne and Wyoming Hotels for many years. The Parkside was made into a bed-and-breakfast around 1980. It is in Ocean City's historic district. Although it has been made into condominiums, the facade remains as it was in earlier days. (Courtesy of OCHM.)

The first large hotel constructed in Ocean City was the Ocean Hotel, built in 1880 by Isaac B. Smith. It was on the corner of Seventh Street and Ocean Avenue, directly on the oceanfront. In 1882, it was sold to Charles Matthews Jr., who changed the name to the Brighton Hotel and hired Richard Risley Sooy to manage it.

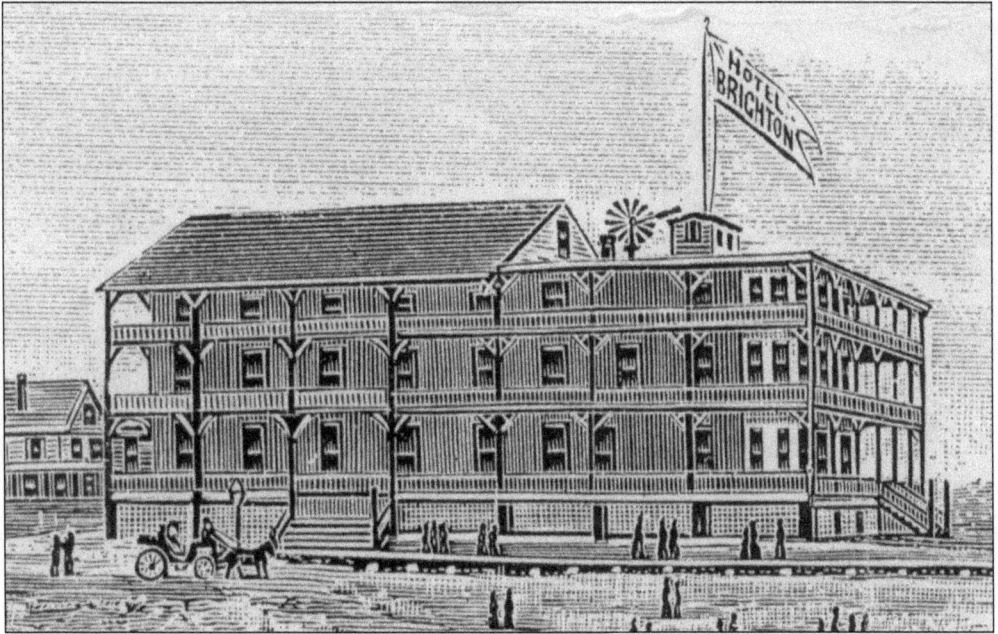

In 1894, Sooy bought the Brighton Hotel. He would own and manage it for over 40 years. Sooy gradually enlarged the hotel until it could accommodate 200 guests. For many years, it was considered the leading hotel in the resort. The Brighton, with an area of 80 feet by 120 feet, was the largest hotel in Ocean City. The building had verandas on each floor.

Around 1900, when this photograph of the Brighton Hotel was taken, it was so close to the beach that people sitting on the verandas frequently were showered with ocean spray. From the upper piazza, known as the "hurricane deck," guests had a wonderful view of Longport and Atlantic City to the north, Great Egg Harbor Bay and its inlets to the west, and the Atlantic Ocean to the east.

As time went on, the beach expanded so much that the Brighton Hotel, which had been built on the beachfront, was eventually two blocks from the ocean. However, it was still one of the most sought-after hotels.

THE BRIGHTON
7th St., Ocean and Atlantic Aves.
OCEAN CITY, NEW JERSEY

In 1940, the Brighton Hotel property was acquired by the city for unpaid taxes. The hotel was then condemned as unsafe and demolished. The city also acquired three vacant lots on Atlantic Avenue adjoining the hotel that had been used for parking. The city put the lots up for sale for residential use. The furniture and all fixtures had been auctioned off before the demolition of the hotel.

15

In 1899, the Hotel Mayberry was built on the corner of Eighth Street and Wesley Avenue, the site of the former Wesley House. By 1901, the Mayberry had been enlarged and refurnished and could accommodate 225 people. It had electric lights, artesian well water, and a long-distance phone.

The name of the Mayberry Hotel was changed to the Wesley Manor in 1915. It was known as the Emeline Hotel from 1938 through the mid 1940s. As the Wesley Arms Hotel, it was a popular hotel from the late 1940s through the 1950s. By 1963, however, the building had fallen into disrepute and was sold and demolished. At the time of this image, the hotel was called the Wesley Arms.

REV. E. B. LAKE'S COTTAGE

Scotch Hall, at 435 Wesley Avenue, was built in 1881 for Ezra B. Lake, one of Ocean City's founders. By 1882, it was known as the Lake Cottage, a guesthouse with eight rooms. In 1910, two women of Scottish heritage bought the house and renamed it Scotch Hall. With a nurse on staff, rooms were rented for "the well, the invalid, and the elderly." During the 1920s, it was a birthing hospital; many of Ocean City's residents were born there. It was later a restaurant. Located in Ocean City's historic district, it is now a private home.

The house at 519 Fifth Street was built in 1882 for Rev. William H. Burrell in the Queen Anne style. When Reverend Burrell lived there, it became known as the "Marrying House," because of the great numbers of weddings he performed there. It was later run as a guesthouse called the Castle Inn, then as a bed-and-breakfast, the New Brighton Inn. Located in the historic district, it is now a private home.

The homes of two of Ocean City's founders can be seen in this photograph taken from the campground. Ezra B. Lake's house, later called Scotch Hall, is right of center. William H. Burrell's house, later called the Castle Inn, is on the left. (Courtesy of Barb and Dean Adams.)

In 1890, Bethany Presbyterian Church members bought a large three-story building on the beach at Thirty-first Street and named it Ocean Rest. According to the church's handbook, their object was "to enable church members to enjoy the benefits of the ocean air at a moderate cost and to enable working people, who could not afford the average high hotel rates, to be able to seek rest at the seashore." Those who could not afford to pay stayed for free. The house had 40 sleeping rooms. A parlor, large dining room, and kitchen, were on the first floor. Wide verandas on two sides of the first and second floors faced the ocean. (Courtesy of Barb and Dean Adams.)

In July 1898, Ocean Rest was sold to the Christian Brothers of Philadelphia, a teaching order of Catholic men. The building (pictured) was used as a retreat by Christian Brothers, who taught in Philadelphia's Catholic schools. In 1906, a second building, housing bedrooms, a chapel, and a lecture room, was added, and in 1914, the original building was enlarged. In 1931, the Brothers began offering classes and tutorials to local students. The buildings were sold in 2013. (Courtesy of Barb and Dean Adams.)

The Emmett Hotel stood on the corner of Eighth Street and Central Avenue, "between the depot and the strand." Built in 1890, the hotel was managed by Mattie Boyle, a teacher in the Ocean City public schools who kept it open all year. In an advertisement in the 1893 *Ocean City Guide Book*, room rates are listed as $1.50 to $2 per day, or $8 to $10 per week. The hotel could accommodate 100 guests. In 1907, the name of the establishment was changed to the Elberon Hotel.

At the Elberon Hotel, every room was "thoroughly heated with hot water heat," and the building had "hot and cold running water in all rooms," according to an advertisement in the *Ocean City Sentinel*. In 1921, the hotel's proprietors were Janet Naylor and Beatrice Sayre. In this photograph, the Elberon Hotel is on the left, and the post office is on the right. (Courtesy of OCHM.)

The Waverly Hotel was on Wesley Avenue below Ninth Street. Built in the late 1890s, it had 75 guest rooms that were rented for the summer season. In 1900, it was managed by Regina Heisler. In 1920, the Waverly was joined with the Hewlings Hotel and renamed the Lincoln Hotel. (Courtesy of Barb and Dean Adams.)

When an auction was held on June 4 and 5, 1920, to sell the Hewlings and Waverly Hotels, the two were bought by Joseph M. Rowland. He remodeled them into one hotel, which he called the Lincoln Hotel. At that time, with 150 rooms, it was one of the largest hotels on the island.

The Lincoln Hotel was on the corner of Ninth Street and Wesley Avenue. Of its 150 rooms, 100 had ocean views. In this image, the part of the hotel that was originally the Hewlings Hotel is on the right, and the former Waverly Hotel is on the left. The Lincoln Hotel was razed on November 20, 1971.

In 1951, the Lincoln Hotel advertised its heated swimming pool as "Ocean City's most beautiful heated pool."

The Lincoln Hotel's restaurant is recommended by *Gourmet* magazine in one of its 1950 issues. The restaurant, which served breakfast, lunch, and dinner, was open to the public.

The Lafayette Hotel was one of Ocean City's most popular and elegant hotels. Built in 1890 on the corner of Central Avenue and Thirteenth Street, it was configured so that almost every room had a view of both the bay and the ocean. The hotel is described in the 1895 *Ocean City Guide Book* as "just far enough back from the high water line on the ocean strand to admit of convenience." In 1921, the hotel's name was changed to the Gladwyn-Lafayette Hotel. It was later called Howard Hall. In this postcard image, the Lafayette Hotel is on the bottom.

Howard Hall had 25 rooms for guests. It was advertised as "near center of town, but away from unpleasant noise . . . over 3,000 square feet of shaded porch area . . . June and September rates half price." Originally called the Lafayette Hotel, it was updated and reopened as Howard Hall in the early 1940s. It is now called the Ambassador Hotel. (Courtesy of OCHM.)

The Arlington Hotel was built at 416 Wesley Avenue in the early 1890s. The three-story hotel could accommodate 75 guests. The proprietors, Beatrix and Edna Heim, prided themselves on their reasonable rates and the cleanliness and friendliness of their service, all of which made the Arlington one of the most sought-after hotels for many years. The structure was torn down in 1980. (Courtesy of Barb and Dean Adams.)

The Traymore Hotel, on the corner of Ninth Street and Wesley Avenue, opened in 1892. It had grounds for lawn tennis and croquet, popular games of the day, and room for 75 guests. The cuisine was "unsurpassed." The Ocean City Electric Trolley ran down Wesley Avenue, making the Traymore's location very convenient. The hotel was destroyed in the fire of October 11, 1927.

The Vandalia House was located at 725 Central Avenue. It opened in 1892 under the management of Mrs. Joseph Burley. The successful hotel saw many guests return year after year. By 1903, the Vandalia House was renamed the Burleigh Hotel. In 1948, it was named the Martha Washington and offered furnished rooms to let. In 1953, it had changed again, and was called the Central Manor and again listed as a hotel.

The Hotel Henry, on the northeast corner of Seventh Street and Asbury Avenue, opened in 1893. In 1921, Oswin H. Henry was the hotel's proprietor. In the late 1920s, the hotel was advertised as the Hotel Henry-Hudson and offered special rates for teachers. The lodging's restaurant was open to the public. The building was later used as a real estate office, a drugstore, and a billiard parlor. It was condemned as unsafe by the Ocean City Building Department in late 1938 and demolished in 1939. (Courtesy of OCHM.)

The Genevieve Guest House was built in 1893 in the Second Empire style, at 615 Wesley Avenue. It had a capacity of 35 guests. In 1924, when Mrs. J. Mann was the manager, rooms could be rented for $20 per week. The building is still used as a guesthouse, although it is now called the Koo-Koo's Nest.

The Hotel White Hall was at 710 Ocean Avenue. Built in 1893, it had 27 rooms and could accommodate 60 people. The guests were served two meals each day, included in the room rate. Its dining room was open to the public. By 1914, the hotel was called the Chandler-White Hall. It was demolished on June 30, 1980.

The Strand Hotel opened in 1894 at Ninth Street and Wesley Avenue. Within one season, a large addition was built, which allowed it to accommodate 125 guests. In 1897, the Strand was owned and managed by R.W. Edwards. By 1900, Milton Cowperthwaite was managing it. He advertised the hotel with this description: "First-class in all its Appointments; Ocean and Bay Views; Electric Lights; Sanitary Plumbing; Artesian Water; Unexcelled Cuisine."

At Ninth Street and Wesley Avenue, the Strand Hotel was perfectly placed to interest visitors. In 1914, the main bridge between Ocean City and the mainland opened on Ninth Street, assuring that all visitors passed the Strand Hotel on their way into and out of the city. The hotel had large verandas, spacious rooms, and "Electric Lights, Private Baths, Liberal Management and Music." The restaurant was open to the public. The hotel was torn down in 1977.

The Atglen Hotel, built in 1895 at Ninth Street and Central Avenue, had a capacity of 100 guests. It was only a few hundred yards from the train station, which, at the time, was the preferred way to get to the island. By the time the Atglen was torn down in 1964 after a fire, its name had been changed to the Surf Hotel. It had been the scene of disorderly conduct arrests and, in 1961, was evacuated after police received an anonymous call that it was to be blown up by a bomb placed in the building.

The Fairview Hotel was built in 1895 on Wesley Avenue near Tenth Street. In 1906, the owner, Albert D. Fogg, enlarged the hotel by an additional 18 rooms and doubled the size of the dining room. Katherine Fizell, the longtime manager of the hotel, advertised "Electric Lights, Pure Water, Perfect Sanitary Arrangements, New Paint."

The Hotel Scarborough was built in 1895 at 720 Ocean Avenue. In 1921, it was advertised as the "Hotel of Courtesy and Service" and had 60 rooms, with a capacity of 75 guests. The hotel is now run as a bed-and-breakfast and is advertised as "An Intimate European-style Inn by the Ocean." It offers free parking on-site and free continental breakfasts.

The Illinois-on-the-Strand Hotel, at 926 Wesley Avenue, opened in 1895. The five-story hotel had 60 guest rooms and a dining room open to the public. It is reported in the July 11, 1895, issue of the *Ocean City Sentinel* that Betsy Ross's granddaughter, Mrs. M.F. Wigert of Fallington, Pennsylvania, was "comfortably settled" at the hotel for the summer and had presented the hotel's owners with a painting of Gen. George Washington, Robert Morris, and Col. George Ross discussing the design of the flag with her grandmother. The hotel was completely destroyed by a fire, believed to be arson, on October 17, 1978.

The Aetna Hotel was built by Anderson Bourgeois in 1896 on the northwest corner of Ninth Street and Ocean Avenue. In 1900, the Ocean City Volunteer Fire Company No. 1 acquired a new Silsby Steam fire engine, the newest, most up-to-date engine available. The firemen held drills the last Thursday of every month. The Aetna Hotel, one of the tallest buildings in the city at the time and only two blocks from the fire station, was the scene of the June 1900 drill. In only two and a half minutes from the time the gong rang, the 10 men on duty had in place a 40-foot ladder reaching to the fourth floor of the hotel, 50 feet of hose unreeled, and water in service.

The Hotel Normandie-on-the-Sea was originally built in 1896 as the Aetna Hotel. It was renamed the Cumberland Hotel in 1907 and, in 1908, Normandie-on-the-Sea. It was on the corner of Ninth Street and Ocean Avenue. With a capacity of 400 guests, it was the largest hotel in Ocean City. The hotel held concerts and other entertainments for the enjoyment of its guests. (Courtesy of OCHM.)

This photograph of the lobby of the Normandie-on-the-Sea Hotel was taken in the early 1900s. The lobby was two stories high, with a grand staircase leading up to balconies. During the day, skylights flooded the area with sunshine. (Courtesy of OCHM.)

The Hotel Normandie-on-the-Sea was destroyed in the fire of October 11, 1927. The blaze, which started in the evening under the boardwalk at Ninth Street, raged for hours, destroying not only the Normandie-on-the-Sea, but also the Traymore Hotel, the Hippodrome Amusement Pier, the Colonial Theatre, and numerous homes, small hotels, and shops. More than 400 firefighters from up and down the coast and from inland towns fought the blaze. Fortunately, thanks to these heroic men, there was no loss of life. Local fire officials and the National Board of Fire Underwriters investigated for months but were unable to determine the fire's cause. In this photograph, taken while the fire was still smoldering, all that is left standing of the Normandie-on-the-Sea is the chimney. (Courtesy of OCHM.)

The Fleetwood Hotel, at Sixth Street and Wesley Avenue, was built in 1896. On May 15, 1922, the hotel, then owned by Mr. and Mrs. Paul Spieker, was completely destroyed by fire. Fortunately, everyone got out safely. The Spiekers rebuilt the hotel after the fire. They opened the new dining room to the public, and the Fleetwood Hotel served its guests well for many years. Today, it is a year-round rooming house. This is a photograph of the rebuilt Fleetwood.

The lobby of the new Fleetwood Hotel had hardwood floors and wicker furniture. There were comfortable chairs in which to sit and read, desks at which to write a quick note, and a piano to play. Guests were welcome to use these amenities. (Courtesy of Barb and Dean Adams.)

The Wyoming Hotel was built in 1896 at 724 Ocean Avenue. With 60 rooms, the hotel was advertised as "near the bathing beach, boardwalk, and all entertainments." It stood next to the Hotel Scarborough, with the Hotel White Hall beyond that. The hotel is now called the Ocean Breeze. (Courtesy of OCHM.)

The Wyoming Hotel was built by Albert P. Milner and was owned for many years by Milner and his wife. It had a capacity of 150 guests. The lobby was a warm, welcoming room that was well used by the hotel's guests. (Courtesy of OCHM.)

The Wyoming Hotel was known for its outstanding cuisine. The dining room was open to the public. (Courtesy of OCHM.)

The Oceanic Hotel, which opened in 1896 at 1114 Wesley Avenue, was open all year. When it was built, it sat amid sand dunes and open land. Nothing was then developed between it and the beach. By 1911, it was advertising "rooms with baths, elevator from street level."

In this photograph of the Oceanic Hotel, taken in the 1930s, the tower has been removed and another story of rooms added. At that time, the hotel had 75 rooms, a capacity of over 200 people, and a public dining room. The building was demolished in 1987. (Courtesy of Barb and Dean Adams.)

The Plymouth Inn, one of the smaller hotels, was built in 1898 and is still an active inn today. When it opened, it offered year-round accommodations with three meals daily. For many years, the Exchange Club, the Rotary Club, and the Lions Club all met here. Today, the Plymouth Inn offers two-bedroom family suites with private baths as well as single rooms and a lavish daily breakfast buffet.

Keith Hall (foreground) was a small hotel at 913–915 Wesley Avenue. Built in the late 1890s, it had 23 rooms for guests. It was located next door to the much larger Traymore Hotel. Although it sustained some damage, Keith Hall survived the October 11, 1927, fire that destroyed the Traymore. In 2005, the building was bought for $1,375,000 and torn down. (Courtesy of OCHM.)

OCEAN CITY
CAPE MAY CO.,
NEW JERSEY
·and its attractions·

·HOTEL DIRECTORY·

AND WHERE TO GO

Price, 10 Cents

In 1900, this directory of Ocean City's hotels and other attractions was published and sold to the public for 10¢. It lists 17 prominent hotels, their locations, size, proprietors, and rates. It also has advertisements for businesses, shops, and services. Also included are photographs of the new boardwalk and some of the important buildings, as well as a map showing the street plan.

The Swarthmore Hotel was built in 1902 at 919–921–923 Wesley Avenue. In 1912, when it was managed by Mrs. Johnson Roney, she advertised "Unobstructed Ocean Views." By the 1940s, the Swarthmore stayed open all year, with much-reduced room rates from late September through late April. It was demolished in May 1985. (Courtesy of Barb and Dean Adams.)

The Sassafras Lodge was built in 1903 at 1145 Central Avenue. It had 11 family-sized rooms and shuffleboard courts and lawn swings for guests. It was open from late May through late September. Now known as the Sassafras Lodge and Hostel, it caters to those on biking excursions.

The Biscayne Hotel, built in 1902 at 812 Ocean Avenue, was only a short walk to the beach and boardwalk. In 1906, advertisements for the Biscayne proclaimed, "Hot Water Heat! Sanitary Conditions Perfect! Private Phones in Rooms!"

The Biscayne Hotel provided such quality accommodations that, in 1911, when New Jersey governor Woodrow Wilson visited Ocean City, he stayed at the hotel.

The solarium of the Biscayne Hotel was filled with sunlight from its large windows. A piano, comfortable seating, and desks were available for use by the hotel's guests. The hotel was demolished in 1989. (Courtesy of Barb and Dean Adams.)

The Biscayne Hotel was purchased in 1919 by Elizabeth and William Blundin. In 1926, they hired Ocean City mayor and prominent builder Joseph G. Champion to redesign and enlarge the building. On the first floor was a spacious lobby with red tile flooring; the second floor contained a large solarium, dining room, and kitchen. Twenty-one rooms were added to the upper floors. In September 1952, the hotel was destroyed by a fire, but the Blundins had it rebuilt and reopened in time for the 1953 summer season.

The Hotel Georgian opened in 1903 at 1120 Central Avenue as the Oxford Hotel. It was later called the Hotel Belmar. In 1940, after remodeling, the hotel was reopened as the Hotel Georgian. It had 30 rooms and a large wraparound porch. In 1944, the hotel was owned by Mabel and William Dotts. During the September 14, 1944, hurricane, the ocean and the bay met in front of the hotel. (Courtesy of Carol and Bill Dotts.)

The lobby of the Hotel Georgian was a spacious, airy room. A brick fireplace was used on chilly evenings, and a bookcase was filled with titles for the guests to enjoy. In the 1954 *Ocean City Directory of Hotels, Guest Homes and Apartments*, the hotel is advertised as having "Special Accommodations for Honeymooners." The hotel received many negative reviews in later years, and it was finally torn down in 2011.

The St. George Hotel opened in 1903 at 609 Eighth Street. Located next to the St. Charles Hotel, it had room for 60 guests. At one time, it was known as the Sherwood Inn and, later, the Beverly. This photograph shows the St. George Inn (left) and the St. Charles. (Courtesy of Barb and Dean Adams.)

# THE BEVERLY

609 Eighth Street

## Ocean City, New Jersey

§ *Where every guest receives* §
§ *..... personal attention .....* §

G. RUSSELL MIDDLETON
Manager

The Beverly Hotel was originally the St. George Hotel. It was advertised as being a place "where every guest receives personal attention." It has been torn down, and the site is now a parking lot. (Courtesy of Barb and Dean Adams.)

45

The Sterling Hotel, on the corner of Eighth Street and Ocean Avenue, opened in 1903. William R. Wick was the proprietor. The Sterling stood next to the St. Charles Hotel. In 1915, the Sterling Hotel's name was changed to the Hotel La Monte. (Courtesy of Barb and Dean Adams.)

The St. Charles Hotel was built in 1903 on Eighth Street between Ocean and Wesley Avenues. Mrs. E.V. Bute was the proprietor. In 1921, the St. Charles and the Hotel La Monte were remodeled into one hotel, reopening as the New Hotel La Monte. (Courtesy of Barb and Dean Adams.)

The New Hotel La Monte, on the corner of Eighth Street and Ocean Avenue, had room for 100 guests. In the April 30, 1926, *Ocean City Sentinel-Ledger*, the hotel is listed for sale by real estate broker Edgar F. Berger. According to the advertisement, "Approximately $50,000 has been spent on this hotel this winter, and it is today one of the best looking, best located and most convenient hotels in Ocean City. Everything that any first-class hotel should have." The price for the hotel is not given. (Courtesy of Barb and Dean Adams.)

After the sale of the New Hotel La Monte, the tower on the roof was removed and stores were added to the first floor.

In the late 1940s, the New Hotel La Monte became the Sandaway Hotel. As the Sandaway, it had 50 rooms, all with running water. Some rooms had private baths. There was a large open porch for guests to enjoy, and individual lockers were provided for patrons to store their beach gear. The building still serves as a hotel, now called the Blue Water Inn.

The Pennsylvania Railroad and YMCA building was at First Street and Bay Avenue. Built in 1905 at the end of a pier, it actually stood over the water. The Pennsylvania Railroad (PRR) had long been a supporter of the Young Men's Christian Association. The PRR YMCA building was used by the railroad's men, who stayed there between runs to Philadelphia and who could bring their families there for vacations. It was also used by the YMCA as a retreat for its members. In 1924, the building was also referred to as PRR YMCA Boys' Seashore Home. (Courtesy of OCHM.)

# *Two*

# LODGING FOR ALL—
# HOTELS, GUESTHOUSES,
# AND APARTMENTS

The publication *Ocean City, NJ Season of 1910* describes Ocean City hotel life thusly:

> Ocean City, most delightful of America's seaside resorts. . . . No matter about the weight of
> your purse, you will find an attractive hotel where an airy, inviting room and wholesome,
> palatable food are to be had. The rainy day loses its usual gloom and dullness in Ocean
> City hotels. No one ever need be lonesome in Ocean City. . . . It's a place where people
> aren't afraid to make the acquaintance of strangers. Dances, hops, card parties, musicals
> and other entertainment held nearly every evening. Exchanges, libraries, writing rooms,
> game rooms, will enable you to find congenial associates and associations.

Apparently, Ocean City's guests agreed with this assessment, as the hotels saw the same guests
returning year after year. Rarely did the lodgings have vacant rooms, and there was a clamor for
more hotels to be built. Between 1906 and the beginning of the Great Depression in October
1929, some 23 additional hotels were constructed, including the Flanders. Some of these hotels
were quite large: the Delaware had room for 400 guests, the Bellevue, 225. Others, such as the
Luray and Ocean Call, were smaller. Room rates and available amenities varied.

An editorial in the May 31, 1929, *Sentinel-Ledger* states, "In the 1927 fire we lost about 25% of our
hotel capacity . . . leaving the city possibly unable to accommodate all who desire to spend their
vacation here. At least two new hotels need to be built each year for the next few years." But the
Great Depression and World War II virtually put a stop to new hotel construction. Guesthouses
and apartments began to take more of the tourism trade. Guesthouses proliferated during the
1940s and early 1950s. The first apartment house built for summer rental was Ocean Court, in
1927. The Sindia Apartments, opened in 1940, were the first to be built on the beach. Hotels with
special amenities continued to do well, as did those that updated their facilities. Other hotels lost
their regular patrons and began to slide into disrepute.

The Modauson, at 34 Corinthian Avenue between First Street and St. James Place, was built in 1905, only 200 feet from the beach. The Georgian Revival mansion got its name from the MOther, DAUghter, and SON who owned and managed it. Unfortunately, their names are unknown. The guesthouse and its public dining room were open from the end of May to October. There were 10 guest rooms with private baths, and bathhouses and showers for use by guests coming from the beach. It was demolished in 2013.

The Hotel Berkeley opened in the early summer of 1906. Built at Forty-eighth Street and Wesley Avenue, it was the first of the large hotels on the south end of Ocean City. The hotel burned to the ground on May 16, 1928. The fire, which was described by the *Ocean City News* as being of mysterious origin, completely destroyed the hotel. At the time of the fire, the hotel, owned by Lloyd Garrett of Philadelphia and John M. Simon of Ocean City, was insured for $20,000. Losses were estimated to be close to $50,000. (Courtesy of Barb and Dean Adams.)

The Imperial Hotel opened in 1906 at 1015 Central Avenue. It was located "two blocks from the beach and boardwalk and two blocks from the train station." In 1944, the name was changed to the Hotel Crest-Mont, and in 1948, it became the Glen-Nor Hotel. In this photograph, taken in July 1906, the Imperial Hotel is on the left. (Courtesy of Barb and Dean Adams.)

The Glen-Nor Hotel had 30 rooms available for summer guests. It was advertised as being "Conveniently Located, Bus Stops at Corner." All of the rooms at the hotel had running water, and some had attached full baths. The Glen-Nor Inn is still in business.

In 1908, the Headam Hotel was built by Ocean City councilmen Harry Headley and George Adams on the corner of Eighth Street and Ocean Avenue. They leased the new hotel to Lawrence & Co. from Pittsburgh, which opened it on Memorial Day 1908. The hotel had 60 rooms, all luxuriantly furnished, many with private baths. From its upper floors, guests had a sweeping view of the ocean. Many prominent families from Pittsburgh stayed at the Headam that summer. In 1909, the hotel was leased to Philadelphian Karl Kemble, who changed the name to the Bellevue Hotel. Kemble enlarged the Bellvue Hotel and kept it open year-round. As the hotel was being readied for demolition in July 2012, a blowtorch sparked a fire that burned for five hours and could be seen for miles around. (Courtesy of OCHM.)

The Bellevue Hotel's swimming pool was enclosed by the walls of the hotel and of nearby buildings, making it very private. The smaller area of the pool was perfect for young children. The two pool slides were fun for the whole family, and the many lounge chairs made for a relaxing visit. Lifeguards were on duty when the pool was open. (Courtesy of Barb and Dean Adams.)

The Hotel Raleigh, at 1008 Wesley Avenue, was built in 1907. A large addition consisting of a palatial front extension and a greatly enlarged dining room was constructed in 1926. Mrs. J. Hamilton and her sons owned and operated the hotel, which was "Homey-Democratic, providing restful happiness and comfort to every guest." It had 50 rooms with a capacity for 100 guests. The hotel was demolished in January 1986. (Courtesy of Barb and Dean Adams.)

In this early photograph, the Hotel Raleigh is the large white building in the center. The addition had not yet been built.

Vernon Hall was built in 1910 at 410 Atlantic Avenue. It operated as a hotel and later as a rooming house. An advertisement for Vernon Hall in a 1923 issue of the *Sentinel-Ledger* declares, "under same management for last seven seasons!" In 2011, the building was torn down. (Courtesy of OCHM.)

The Lorraine Hotel stood at 841 Central Avenue. A 1911 advertisement described the Lorraine as "high class, moderate rates, with home comforts, service and cuisine unexcelled." The hotel, with accommodations for 100 guests, was managed by Frances L. Deisroth. By 1915, the hotel was called the Kentucky House. (Courtesy of OCHM.)

The Kentucky House, originally the Lorraine Hotel, opened in 1915. There was a real estate office on the ground floor, with rooms for guests on the upper three stories. In 1938, the name was changed to the Elida Hotel.

The owners of the Elida Hotel used the first floor as a restaurant offering both American and German food to their guests and to the public. The upper floors contained rooms for the hotel guests. The building was later used as a restaurant and is currently the office of a local architect. The Elida Hotel had previously operated as the Lorraine Hotel and then the Kentucky House. (Courtesy of Barb and Dean Adams.)

The Breakers Hotel, on the boardwalk at Delancey Place between Second and Third Streets, was the first hotel built on the boardwalk. It opened on June 29, 1912 with a gala dinner and reception attended by many prominent Ocean City and Philadelphia businessmen and their wives. The hotel offered unobstructed views of the beach and ocean from its veranda and from many of its rooms. It was torn down in November 1970.

In 1913, the Sindia Guest House opened at 801 Plymouth Place, on the corner of Atlantic Avenue. It was named for the four-masted bark *Sindia*, which ran aground on the beach at Seventeenth Street on December 15, 1901. In 1928, George Cohick purchased the building and opened a restaurant serving Pennsylvania Dutch food. Today, the restaurant offers breakfast and dinner, but the building no longer operates as a guesthouse. (Courtesy of Barb and Dean Adams.)

Chelten Manor was built in 1903 at 1030 Ocean Avenue, along what was known as "Millionaires Row." It was a large summer home built for the T.C. McCann family of suburban Philadelphia. By the 1930s, it was being used as a guesthouse, first as the Rutherford, then as the Sandborg, and later as Chelten Manor. The house is still standing, although it is in disrepair.

The Ocean Manor, at 1040 Ocean Avenue, was built as a private home for the A. McCann family in 1903, across from the beach. In the early 1920s, the city planned a joint public/private venture to build a hotel on the property directly across the street. This would become the Flanders Hotel. For the next few years, McCann fought the construction of the new hotel, to no avail. It was said that he and his family abandoned the house, never to return. In the early 1950s, the property was restored and opened as a guesthouse with 25 rooms. It is still in use today.

The Alvyn Hotel opened in 1914 at 814 Brighton Place, between Fourth and Fifth Streets. It was very near the beach and had 46 rooms with a capacity of 100 guests. The hotel advertisements declared, "An Adventure in Delightful Living" and "Planned for Perfect Pleasure." The dining room, known for its outstanding cuisine and excellent service, was open to the public and could serve 350 people at each sitting. The hotel was torn down in 1979.

The Comfort Inn, at 210 Bay Avenue, was directly on the bay, opposite the steamboat landing. It was owned and operated by Rev. Samuel J. Comfort, pastor of the Tabernacle Baptist Church, and his wife. When Booker T. Washington, the most prominent African American leader and educator of the day, came to Ocean City to speak at the First Methodist Episcopal Church on September 9, 1914, he stayed with the Comforts at their hotel.

The Comfort Inn had a café where guests could enjoy dinners and light lunches, including 50¢ dinners. In the early evening, ice cream and confectioneries were also served. The café was open to the public as well as to the hotel's guests. When Booker T. Washington visited Ocean City in 1914, a luncheon was held in his honor at the café. (Courtesy of Barb and Dean Adams.)

The Carpenter Guest House, owned and managed by John Carpenter, opened in 1917 at 3128 Central Avenue. In this photograph, the Carpenter Guest House is in the background at center. A group of bathers, some of whom may have been staying at the Carpenter, pose in front of a lifeboat. The lifeguards surrounding the unknown woman in the white dress are, from left to right, Henry M. Dibbs, Capt. William Seaman, and C. Van Dyke Conover.

The Luray Hotel, at 636 Wesley Avenue, had 35 rooms, and its "beautiful second floor dining room" was open to the public. The room rates were available with or without meals. In 1924, the advertisements described the Luray as "a summer home for those who appreciate a refined, homelike atmosphere. Moderately priced . . . [it is] near to every activity yet in a quiet section." (Courtesy of Barb and Dean Adams.)

The Alden Park Manor was at 915 Fourth Street, overlooking the ocean at Fourth Street. It was open only during the summer season, from May until October. The manor had 27 rooms and a few small apartments. There were three large porches fronting the building and a spacious lounge with a large fireplace. Alden Park Manor had "Frigidaire drinking water." (Courtesy of Barb and Dean Adams.)

In 1938, a calisthenics class was conducted on the roof of the Alden Park Manor. Organized by summer vacationers, the class was held every afternoon. Apparently, the morning exercise class held on the beach each day by Elmer E. Unger was not enough!

The Hostess House for Convalescent Girls stood at 940 Central Avenue. The first Hostess House was a small store on the boardwalk rented by a group of Philadelphia women during World War I as a place where servicemen could come for rest and recuperation. In 1922, when the government started providing this for the men, the facility was opened to young working women. When the facility outgrew the store on the boardwalk, it moved first to 416–418 Ocean Avenue and then to the house on Central Avenue. Its mission was to "help sick working girls, whether they could pay or not, back to good health through sea breezes, wholesome food, and companionship." The directors conducted an annual "mile-of-dimes" drive on the boardwalk to support the house. In 1972, the Hostess House was deeded to Shore Memorial Hospital, across the bridge in Somers Point, New Jersey.

The Ocean City Seashore Home for Babies was established on July 11, 1922. A group of Philadelphia women bought the old Yacht Club building at Sixth Street and Pleasure Avenue, with the intention to "house babies and children of impoverished families from the inner city during the summer, and to give the children a chance to grow strong and healthy with the aid of good food, sea air, and salt water." Local doctors offered their services gratis, and nursing staff cared for the children. During that summer, the women held a fund drive to help pay for the building. For several years after, the women were in charge of the annual baby parade, with the entrance fees and freewill offerings used to help support the home. (Courtesy of OCHM.)

The Hotel Moorlyn View consisted of six buildings—816, 818, and 820 Ocean Avenue, and 711, 713, and 715 Moorlyn Terrace. Moorlyn Terrace ends at Ocean Avenue, and the buildings were, therefore, very close to or adjacent to each other. This photograph shows the Ocean Avenue structures. The buildings on Moorlyn Terrace were advertised as the "Shady Side Annex." Altogether, the hotel had 50 rooms available for guests.

This 1922 photograph, with a view looking south along Ocean Avenue, was taken from the sixth floor of the Bellevue Hotel. On the right can be seen, from front to rear, the Biscayne Hotel, the Moorlyn View Hotel, and the Normandie-on-the-Sea Hotel. (Courtesy of Rahn G. Brackin.)

The Hotel Delaware was built in 1925 on the boardwalk at Third Street. Constructed entirely of brick, the hotel's five stories were built to be fireproof. On June 26, 1925, the Hotel Delaware was formally opened with a dinner for 150 members of the Ocean City Chamber of Commerce. Lauded as one of the best-appointed hotels along the Atlantic coast, it had 100 rooms, half with private baths. Every room commanded a view of the ocean. (Courtesy of Barb and Dean Adams.)

In 1929, a $150,000 addition to the Hotel Delaware added 75 rooms. The capacity of the hotel went from 250 to 400 guests. Sun parlors were located at the end of the two wing extensions, and a special dining room for families with children was also added. Calvin Anderson, the hotel's owner, is lauded in the June 7, 1929, *Sentinel-Ledger*: "Calvin Anderson, in enlarging the Delaware has given to Ocean City another invaluable asset. It is a monument of faith in the sound, steady progress of the resort, and of its constantly growing attraction for summer visitors." This photograph shows the Hotel Delaware after the addition. (Courtesy of Barb and Dean Adams.)

On February 19, 1948, one of the worst fires in Ocean City's history occurred at the Hotel Delaware. The local fire stations were short of equipment, as two of the city's fire engines were out of service. It took the help of stations from Atlantic City and elsewhere to bring the fire under control. This photograph shows the rebuilt Hotel Delaware after the fire. The hotel was demolished in October 1971.

The Ocean Call was a small hotel on Central Avenue just below Fourteenth Street. Built in the mid-1920s, it offered guests the opportunity to use the hotel's cooking facilities. Individual stoves, refrigerators, and lockers for food storage were available to the guests. The management served a "club breakfast." Each room, while not having a private bath, did have hot and cold running water. (Courtesy of Barb and Dean Adams.)

The Southern Hotel was at 835 Fifth Street, across from the playing fields and less than half a block from the boardwalk and beach. There were 30 rooms available for guests, some single, some adjoining. The dining room, which was open to the public, allowed guests to enjoy all three meals at the hotel.

In 1926, the Southern Hotel was enlarged and completely renovated. The addition consisted of five stories at the rear of the building, making room for a new kitchen, a larger dining room, and an additional 22 guest rooms. The addition can be seen on the left in this photograph. The hotel was known as the Center Court Hotel when it burned to the ground in 1985. In the blaze, an adjacent home was also destroyed and another building was heavily damaged. (Courtesy of Barb and Dean Adams.)

HALCYON HALL
1116 WESLEY AVE.
OCEAN CITY, N. J.

HARRISON OWNERSHIP
MANAGEMENT

Halcyon Hall, at 1116 Wesley Avenue, had 28 guest rooms. In 1924, when Felicia D. Maxwell was the proprietor, she advertised "airy, comfortable rooms, each with running water. We are located near beach, boardwalk and all recreational activities, and have free bathing from the hotel with showers and lockers." Halcyon Hall could comfortably house 100 guests.

The building at 601 Atlantic Avenue was constructed for Rev. James E. Lake in 1910. He and his wife rented the house to guests for several summer seasons. On May 13, 1927, they sold the property to Edmund and Martha Holcroft, who named it Croft Hall and ran it as a guesthouse, with 29 rooms for paying guests. One block from the beach and boardwalk, the building was close to good restaurants and near the recreation department's tennis and basketball courts and track. In 2003, Croft Hall was totally renovated and reopened as the Atlantis Bed and Breakfast Inn.

The oceanfront Bristol Hotel offered guests hot and cold running water in all rooms, free parking, and bathing from the hotel. Located at 1432 Ocean Avenue, it opened in mid-May for the summer season. It was touted as being "conveniently located near all social and vacation activities."

The Ocean Court Apartments opened in 1927 at 300 Ocean Avenue. The apartments were rented throughout the summer to families by the weekend, week, or month. These were the first apartments to be rented out short-term during the summer. This approach later became quite common. The apartments were later sold as cooperatives and remain that way today.

French Cottage, on the corner of Moorlyn Terrace and Ocean Avenue, was one block down Moorlyn Terrace from the popular Music Pier, where daily public concerts were held. Opened in 1928 by Florence B. French, who was both the owner and manager of the guesthouse, French Cottage stayed open all year and offered meals to the guests. Beginning in 1953, it was known as the Haddon Cottage. (Courtesy of Barb and Dean Adams.)

The Washington Hotel, at 12 East Sixth Street near Simpson Avenue, had an African American clientele. The hotel advertises in the *1933 Guide and Information Booklet* that it has rooms, a dormitory, and offers meals and refreshments at moderate rates. It had running water in every room and à la carte service. The dining room was open to the public. (Courtesy of OCHM.)

The Hanscom Hotel, at Eighth Street just off the boardwalk, opened on July 22, 1929, as "Ocean City's New Modern, Fireproof Hotel." Built of brick and limestone by Melvin Hanscom and his sons, the Hanscom was "an elegant hotel near the beach and boardwalk offering first-class accommodations for those of moderate means." The building contractor was D.A. McClelland of Philadelphia, who earlier had built the Flanders Hotel. In 1968, a group of Philadelphia Methodists bought the building, remodeled it, renamed it the Homestead, and opened it as a home for senior citizens. In 2005, the building was redone again. Individual units were sold as condominiums, and it now functions as the Homestead Condominium Hotel. (Courtesy of Barb and Dean Adams.)

The Hanscoms, who built the Hanscom Hotel, were well-known Philadelphia bakers and restaurateurs with an excellent reputation for exquisite cuisine. At the hotel, they offered fine dining at a restaurant on the premises that was also open to the public. In 1929, full-course dinners cost between 64¢ and $1.50.

Posing here are the young women who waited tables in the Hanscom Hotel restaurant in 1934. The 26 women received free room and board in a large cottage. A housemother made sure they were all in the cottage by 12:30 a.m., did not smoke, and kept their rooms neat. Before their shifts started, they had to put on clean, starched uniforms and hairnets and make sure their stocking seams were straight. In the first row, fourth from left, is Myrtle Connelly, hostess of the group. In the third row, second from left, is her sister, Gertrude Connelly. The other women are unidentified. (Courtesy of OCHM.)

A solarium was built on the roof of the Hanscom Hotel. From there, guests could enjoy a view of the beach, ocean, and cityscape. A large roof garden and deck could be accessed from the solarium. Guests used the sunny room for card playing, reading, and relaxing. Both the solarium and the dining room were popular draws for the hotel. (Courtesy of Barb and Dean Adams.)

The Colonial Hotel was a beachfront establishment at 831 Atlantic Avenue. Built in 1929, it was advertised as having "no streets to cross going to boardwalk or beach, good restaurants and dining rooms nearby." (Courtesy of Barb and Dean Adams.)

In 1950, an apartment was added to the front of the Colonial Hotel. At that time, the owners advertised the following: "All Outside Rooms and Florida Type Apartment, Running Water, Innerspring Mattresses, Convenient to All Restaurants and Stores." The Colonial Hotel was demolished in the spring of 1979.

The Brighton-Atlantic Apartments, on the corner of Atlantic Avenue and Brighton Place, rented furnished apartments by the week, month, or season during the summer. Opened for the summer of 1931, they were one block from the beach. The units, constructed to be fireproof and soundproof, had hardwood floors, hot water at all times, and telephone outlets. The building was entirely insulated, to keep it cool during the summer heat. The units are now individually owned and, if rented, are rented yearly.

The Princeton Inn was at Third Street and Corinthian Avenue. From the 1930s through the 1950s, it offered furnished rooms and small apartments for rent by the week, month, or season during the summer. The former Princeton Inn is now a private home. (Courtesy of Barb and Dean Adams.)

When Clayton Haines Brick, vice president of the Ocean City Title & Trust Co. and former president of the Ocean City Chamber of Commerce, died unexpectedly in 1938, his wife was forced to open her home to paying guests. Mary Brick ran the Brick Guest House at 920 Wesley Avenue. She offered her guests free parking. The house was torn down in March 1986. (Courtesy of Barb and Dean Adams.)

The Nassau, at 1444–1446 Ocean Avenue, offered efficiency, one-, two-, and three-bedroom apartments, described as "Deluxe, Modern, Beach Front." Open from May through September, the Nassau was located across the street from a lifeguarded beach and was near churches, stores, and the boardwalk. It attracted many families who returned year after year. (Courtesy of Barb and Dean Adams.)

The Sindia Apartments, opened in 1940 at Eighteenth Street and the boardwalk, was a new concept for summer visitors. Although there were other apartments for summer let, only the Sindia's 40 apartments were built directly on the beach, specifically for summer rentals. Each unit consisted of two bedrooms, a living room–dining room combination, a small kitchen, and a bathroom. They were completely furnished except for silverware, linens, and blankets. The Sindia Apartments was named for the bark *Sindia*, which came ashore in a storm in December 1901 a block from where the apartments were later built. For many years, the mast of the ship could be seen from the beach. The apartments were razed in 1987.

The Marbildotom was a guesthouse run by the Kingsley family. Built over the water at the end of a pier at 428 Bay Avenue, it was named for the Kingsley children—Marsha, Bill, Don, and Tom. It had eight guest rooms and was operated on the European plan. The Marbildotom catered to those who had boats docked nearby. (Courtesy of Barb and Dean Adams.)

The Corcoran House was on Ocean Avenue at Fourth Street. In 1942, it was the first guesthouse seized by the US Coast Guard during World War II for use as a sleeping dormitory for its men. After the war, it resumed its use as a guesthouse. Under the ownership and management of Dolly and Bernie Corcoran, the guesthouse had large rooms, each with a private bath. The dining room was open to the public.

The Mir-A-Mar Hotel was a popular inn at 929 Fourth Street, directly on the beach, behind the boardwalk. On September 14, 1944, the worst hurricane to hit Ocean City destroyed the Mir-A-Mar and caused hundreds of thousands of dollars in damage throughout the city. Fortunately, there was no loss of life. The hurricane occurred after the summer season had ended and most seasonal visitors had left. In these photographs, taken after the hurricane, the Mir-A-Mar is the building on the right. In the photograph below, the boardwalk can be seen on the left. The hurricane had wind speeds of 96 miles per hour. The day before the storm, the weather bureau had downgraded the wind expectations, from 100 miles per hour to 55–70 miles per hour. It was expected to pass Ocean City 100 miles out to sea, but it actually got within 47 miles of the coast.

The Berkshire Guest House was at 705 Ocean Avenue. An advertisement in a 1944 *Sentinel-Ledger* proclaims, "When in Ocean City looking after your property or taking a few days vacation . . . come to the Berkshire Guest House and *really* enjoy your stay!" (Courtesy of Barb and Dean Adams.)

Jernee Manor, on the corner of Thirty-sixth Street and Central Avenue, was built in 1899 as a US Life-Saving Service station. In 1946, it was bought from the federal government by Jack Jernee, a former captain of the Ocean City Beach Patrol, after he retired from the Navy in 1945. Jernee and his family operated the property as a guesthouse for many years before selling it in 1981, when it was torn down. Members of the beach patrol unsuccessfully tried to save the building from demolition. (Courtesy of OCHM.)

The Bryn Mawr was at 824 Wesley Avenue. In the 1930s and 1940s, the 800 block of Wesley Avenue was known as "Doctor's Row" because of the many physicians who had offices there. From 1948 to 1964, Dr. John B. Townsend had his office on the first floor of the building. The upper floors were used as the Bryn Mawr Guest House, with 20 rooms for guests. It was advertised as "The Family Home with a Christian Atmosphere." (Courtesy of OCHM.)

The Ocean View Hotel and Apartments, at 850 Plymouth Place, had hotel rooms as well as family-sized apartments consisting of two bedrooms, a small kitchen, a living room, and a bathroom. Only a half-block from a lifeguarded beach, the Ocean View's location and family-friendly size made it very attractive. Many families returned to the Ocean View year after year. (Courtesy of Barb and Dean Adams.)

The Maryellen Guest House was at 815 Fifth Street, across from the recreation park. Maryellen Wiegel was the owner and manager of the property. Foam rubber mattresses were installed in the rooms and in the four-bedroom apartment. The apartment, which could sleep 10, had an electric kitchen. It could be rented by the week, month, or season; the rooms were also let daily.

The Franklin Guest House, at 621 Ocean Avenue, had 12 rooms for guests. Mr. and Mrs. E.P. Bechtel were longtime owners/ managers of the guesthouse. They lived in Collegeville, Pennsylvania, during the off-season. They advertised their guesthouse as having a "Pleasant Home Atmosphere, Centrally Located, Near the Boardwalk."

Penny's Hotel, at 1402–1404 Ocean Avenue, was actually a guesthouse. In 1953, it was remodeled, and bathrooms were added to each room. Its second-floor veranda overlooked the beach, ocean, and boardwalk. There was a spacious, luxurious lobby for the guests to enjoy, and the rooms were newly furnished. Outside showers were available for use by the guests after spending the day on the beach.

The Ebbie Cottage, at 820 Sixth Street, was owned and managed by Mrs. George Ebner, who kept its 10 rooms open all year. It had hot and cold water in all bedrooms and offered bathhouses for guests coming from the beach, which was only one block away. It was advertised as "overlooking the glittering Beach and Ocean . . . and Proximity to the Modern Boardwalk, and Center of Amusements . . . offers you a Clean, Invigorating Atmosphere and Vacation." (Courtesy of Barb and Dean Adams.)

The Manor was a guesthouse at 730 Moorlyn Terrace near Atlantic Avenue. It was one block from the beach, the boardwalk, the Music Pier, and the bus terminal. The Manor, open from May through September, had 19 rooms for guests. It was advertised as being "close to many good restaurants."

Spruce Lodge, at 1406 Ocean Avenue, across the street from the beach, had an unobstructed view of the ocean. Its nine rooms and two small, ground-floor apartments could be rented weekly or monthly during the summer season. It was advertised as "always cool, comfortable and friendly." (Courtesy of Barb and Dean Adams.)

The Walton Guest House stood at 701 Ocean Avenue. Its small, furnished apartment on the ground floor was also available for rent during the summer season. Only one block from the beach, the Walton had bathhouses with hot and cold showers available for the guests. Special rates were offered for June and September. (Courtesy of Barb and Dean Adams.)

The Vernon Guest House was at 1228 Ocean Avenue. Owned and managed by William H. and Grace M. Vernon, it had a strong family atmosphere. Directly across from the beach, the Vernon was much in demand every summer.

# *Three*

# FLANDERS, JEWEL OF THE SOUTHERN JERSEY SHORE

For several years, residents had discussed the need for a new, modern oceanfront hotel as a necessity if Ocean City was to keep up with its resort rivals. The chamber of commerce appointed a committee to look into the matter, and it came to the same conclusion.

In 1922, a group of Ocean City businessmen decided to make that need a reality, planning an elegant oceanfront hotel on the boardwalk at Eleventh Street. It would be the largest construction project ever undertaken in the city. The hotel was to have 150 feet fronting the boardwalk and 285 feet fronting Eleventh Street. There would also be some frontage on Ocean Avenue, which would allow for store rentals and concessions within the hotel grounds. The new hotel was to be called the Flanders, after Belgium's Flanders Field, where many American servicemen were buried. It was felt that this hotel would have a great influence on lengthening the summer season and would help Ocean City become a year-round resort.

The Ocean Front Hotel Corporation of Ocean City, New Jersey, was composed of prominent businessmen and civic leaders. William E. Massey, president of the Ocean City Title & Trust Company, was general chairman; Joseph M. Rowland, owner of the Lincoln Hotel, was vice chairman; and former mayor Harry Headley was treasurer. They were tasked with constructing and operating the hotel and allowing shareholders to participate in and fully share in the profits. The project was to be "a project of the community, by the community, and for the community, and every resident of the community, both permanent and summer," would be given the opportunity to purchase stock at par value of $100 per share. The hotel opened on July 28, 1923, to much fanfare. Over the years, the Flanders Hotel has been the most photographed building in Ocean City and has been pictured in more postcards than anything else in the city. It has served the city well, as both a meeting place and a venue for memorable events. The lodging, in the National Register of Historic Places, now operates as an all-suite luxury hotel.

Ocean Front Hotel Corporation

Incorporated under the Laws of the State of New Jersey

This Certifies that Bertram M. Darby is the owner of Two Shares of One Hundred Dollars each of the Capital Stock of Ocean Front Hotel Corporation transferable only on the books of the Corporation by the holder hereof in person or by Attorney upon surrender of this Certificate properly endorsed.

In Witness Whereof, the said Corporation has caused this Certificate to be signed by its duly authorized officers and to be sealed with the Seal of the Corporation this 15th day of September A.D. 1923.

NUMBER 329        2 SHARES

SHARES $100 EACH

The Ocean Front Hotel Corporation sold shares in the corporation to both permanent and summer residents at a par value of $100 per share. This certificate is for two shares sold to Bertram M. Darby on September 15, 1923. Darby was a permanent resident of Ocean City and a local historian. For many years, he was a member of the Cape May County Board of Taxation.

Ocean City native Vivian B. Smith was appointed architect of the project. He had designed Ocean City's city hall, built in 1914. He later went on to design Ocean City's high school and Music Pier, as well as Ventnor City's city hall. The hotel was to have approximately 250 rooms, public and private dining rooms, club rooms, banquet rooms and ballrooms, lounges, gardens, stores, and exclusive shops.

The Ocean Front Hotel Corporation and architect Vivian Smith chose David McClelland of Philadelphia to build the Spanish Mission Revival hotel. It was to be constructed of steel girders and a new, non-Portland cement, with a red tile roof. The building was planned to be completely fireproof. The structure had rounded focal windows and square towers. This photograph was taken on April 21, 1923; just three months later, the hotel was ready for its grand opening.

The hotel was to feature steam heat, freshwater and salt water in all the lavatories, and two elevators. The decoration was opulent. This photograph, taken on July 26, 1923, shows the hotel facade, not yet completed, fronting the boardwalk and beach.

# The Flanders

## Ocean City, New Jersey

### American Plan

A new, fireproof structure of 232 rooms, each with lavatory,
toilet and bath facilities. Thoroughly modern, beautifully appointed and has an ideal location directly on the Boardwalk at
Eleventh Street. All outside rooms. Two large lobbies, ball
room, dining rooms and writing rooms. Two passenger and
service elevators. Solariums. Open and closed porches provide
400 feet of ocean and southern exposure. Sunken Garden where
refreshments will be served from The Flanders' Fountain on the
Boardwalk and from where the aquatic sports in the pool may be
watched. Fine open-air pool and Bath Department with lockers.
Hot and cold sea water baths. Golf, tennis, riding, swimming,
yachting, fishing and other outdoor sports.

Rates on Application.

J. HOWARD SLOCUM, Pres.-Mgr.
For seven years Manager, "The Greenbrier," White Sulphur
Springs, West Virginia

This advertisement, in the Ocean City Fishing Club's 1923 yearbook, touts the many features of
the Flanders: "A new fireproof structure of 232 rooms each with private lavatories. . . . Thoroughly
modern, beautifully appointed. . . . Two large lobbies, ballroom, dining rooms and writing rooms.
. . . Sunken Garden where refreshments will be served . . . and from where the aquatic sports in
the pool may be watched." The hotel would be on the American plan, serving guests three meals
a day. J. Howard Slocum, who had managed the Greenbrier Inn in White Sulphur Springs, West
Virginia, for seven years, was the manager of the new hotel.

On Saturday evening, July 28, 1923, over 400 people attended the grand opening of the Flanders Hotel. The evening was stormy, and the hotel was not completely finished, but the formal dinner had been well publicized and was attended not only by members of the Ocean Front Hotel Corporation and their wives, but also by stockholders and prominent citizens from both Ocean City and Philadelphia. Newspapers in New York City, Philadelphia, and Washington, DC, carried the news of the opening and the gala evening. This pen-and-ink drawing of the Flanders Hotel is on the cover of the gala's program.

The main dining room of the Flanders Hotel was formally set for the dinner on the night of the gala opening. The women were magnificently gowned, and the men were dressed in formal evening wear. The dinner was a great success. Thomas F. Armstrong presided as toastmaster. (Courtesy of Barb and Dean Adams.)

# MENU

FRUIT CUP, FAVORITE

SALTED ALMONDS                    OLIVES

CONSOMME YVETTE

AIQUILETTE OF STRIPED BASS, ADMIRAL

POTATOES HOLLANDAISE

SADDLE OF SPRING LAMB

NEW PEAS, FRENCH STYLE

PUNCH PARFAIT D'AMOUR

SUPREME OF CHICKEN MOUSSELINE

HEARTS OF LETTUCE

MOUSSE GLACE FLANDERS

ASSORTED CAKES

COFFEE

This is the menu from the gala opening dinner. Featured were striped bass, saddle of spring lamb, potatoes hollandaise, supreme of chicken mousseline, and mousse glace Flanders.

The swimming pool at the Flanders Hotel opened on Memorial Day 1924, ten months after the hotel itself opened. The pool was surrounded on three sides by the hotel, making it very private for the hotel guests. A fountain adorned the terrace, where tables, chairs, and umbrellas were set out. Guests could have lunch served there. A lifeguard was on duty whenever the pool was open.

To celebrate the May 30, 1924, opening of the swimming pool at the Flanders Hotel, the members of the Ambassador Club's swim team put on an aquatic exhibition. They continued to put on water-sports shows there every Friday evening throughout that summer.

Locksley Hall was a large rooming house built in 1911 by Charles A. Doe at Eleventh Street and the boardwalk. In November 1922, the building was moved north, adjacent to where the Flanders Hotel was being constructed. For 70 years, Locksley Hall was used as a men's dormitory for the staff of the Flanders Hotel. The property was bought in 1996 by Scott Simpson, who razed the building to enlarge his Playland Amusement Park. In the 1940s, the Larchmont Hotel, at 1100 Ocean Avenue, was used as a women's dormitory. (Courtesy of OCHM.)

Jimmy Stewart, one of the best-known actors of the 1950s, came to Ocean City with his family from Indiana, Pennsylvania, when he was a child and young man. When he visited the Flanders Hotel in 1991, he told a reporter for the *Ocean City Sentinel-Ledger* that he remembered spending many afternoons swimming in the Flanders pool as a youngster.

On Saturday, June 7, 1924, this publicity photograph was taken near the Flanders Hotel. Mayor Joseph G. Champion, pointing to the sign, shows the swim team from the Ambassador Club the city's slogan, "America's Greatest Family Resort."

The Flanders received so much attention and was so well known throughout the country that a picture of the hotel was used in this advertisement in the March 12, 1925, *Engineering News-Record*. The type of floor construction featured here was used throughout the hotel's 120,000 square feet. It was available from the General Fireproofing Company of Youngstown, Ohio.

From one of the outdoor solariums, Flanders Hotel guests could enjoy the sea breezes and sunshine while watching the crowd on the boardwalk go by. In this photograph, the building on the right is the Hippodrome Pier, at Ninth Street. The beach patrol headquarters is visible on the beach at Tenth Street. Both buildings were destroyed in the fire of October 11, 1927.

This scene from the summer of 1925 shows the beach and boardwalk as they extend in front of the Flanders Hotel. Because the beach had grown so large, after the boardwalk fire of October 11, 1927, the boardwalk was moved forward, toward the ocean.

The 1925 *Ocean City Guide Book* includes this photograph of the exercise classes held each morning on the beach near the Flanders Hotel. W. Ward Beam, a well-known instructor from Philadelphia, led the classes. The article describes the great appeal of Ocean City for those visitors who were "athletically inclined." The beach exercise classes, municipal tennis courts, and Flanders pool are all touted. The Flanders Hotel is the large building in the background at left.

This photograph appears in the September 11, 1925, *Ocean City Sentinel-Ledger*. The caption read as follows: "Members of W. Ward Beam's 'Daily Dozen' health exercise class having a little workout on the beach in front of the Flanders Hotel."

This 1925 photograph of the Flanders Hotel shows the statues of Greek gods, dolphins, and gargoyles that adorned the hotel. In the foreground, Ocean City lifeguard William Stevens poses for a photograph with three unidentified women.

This 1928 photograph, taken in the spring, shows the boardwalk being rebuilt after the fire of October 11, 1927. The new construction used concrete beams, girders, and support pilings, the first boardwalk in the country to do so. The new boardwalk extended from Sixth Street to Twelfth Street. The Flanders Hotel is the large building on the right.

In this photograph, taken in the summer of 1928, the distance between the newly rebuilt boardwalk and the Flanders Hotel can be seen. The Flanders Hotel management built a wooden walkway to connect the hotel to the new boardwalk. (Courtesy of Barb and Dean Adams.)

June 28, 1929, was the fifth and final day of the eighth annual National Marble Tournament, held at the Flanders Hotel. It was the first time the event had been held in Ocean City. First prize was a trip to Ocean City and a stay at the Flanders Hotel for the winner and his family. An article in the *Pittsburgh Press* declares, "Shining in the Ocean City sunlight like the white palace of an old time king, the Flanders Hotel, home of luxury and ease, awaits the coming of the modern kings of American boydom—The Marble Champions of America." Shown here is the champion, Charles "Sonny" Albany, 13, of Philadelphia.

In 1929, three saltwater pools were built by the Flanders management in the space between the hotel and the new boardwalk. The main pool was Olympic-sized and chest-deep; a smaller, deeper pool was used for diving; and a children's pool, about 18 inches deep, was for the littlest bathers.

These new pools were open to the public for a small fee. A large bathhouse was available for people to change and shower. By noon, the pools were crowded. On a hot day, there were as many as 1,500 people in the pool area.

The hotel employed more than 30 trained instructors and lifeguards, who were on duty daily. In addition to protecting the bathers, these men and women taught swimming. During instruction, a sign reading "Instruction Area, Please Keep Out" was posted to keep other swimmers away from the area. It has been said that every Ocean City resident learned to swim in the Flanders Hotel pools.

# WARNING!

## Tuesday Night, August 6th, 7:30 sharp

Harry H. Gardiner, the World's Famous Human Fly, pioneer of unexplored daredevil trials and reported dead many times, at 7.30 sharp will scale the Hotel Flanders, corner of 11th street and Boardwalk. He will start the climb at the sidewalk, climb up and over the roof and back down to the street again without any mechanical aid.

A band concert will be given at 7 o'clock to entertain the early arrivals.

You are cordially invited to witness this gigantic thrill.

The performance is under the Auspices and for the Benefit of the Cape May County American Legion Band and Morgan-Ranck Post, No 137.

(Do Not Read Other Side)

On August 6, 1929, Harry H. Gardiner, the "World Famous Human Fly, pioneer of unexplored daredevil trials and reported dead many times," was to scale the Flanders Hotel. He was to start his ascent at the sidewalk, climb up and over the roof, and climb back down to the street. The stunt was to benefit the Cape May County American Legion Band and Morgan-Ranck Post No. 137. This poster was used to advertise the event. Gardiner successfully climbed up the Flanders, but he injured his wrist on the roof and was unable to climb back down.

At the time of this 1930 photograph, guests could pick up mail and room keys from the exchange desk in the second-floor lobby. From the exchange, guests could walk down a hall to the solariums, down another opulent hall to the dining rooms, and from there, down a set of curved stairs to the patio dining room overlooking the original swimming pool. When the hotel was built, this was the center of the entire resort. (Courtesy of Barb and Dean Adams.)

Future movie actress Grace Kelly was just a baby when her family began visiting Ocean City from their home in Philadelphia. The family built a summer home at 2536 Wesley Avenue in 1931. They stayed at the Flanders Hotel while the house was being completed. In this photograph, taken in the lobby of the Flanders, Grace (center) poses with her brother Jack and her sister Margaret.

By 1932, the Flanders Hotel was being affected by the Great Depression. The hotel had made considerable money for its bondholders until 1930, when it began to lose money. In November 1932, J. Howard Slocum, manager of the hotel, and New Jersey state senator Charles C. Read, were appointed receivers of the Ocean Front Hotel Corporation, owner of the Flanders. In 1933, the corporation sold the hotel to Elwood Kirkman (shown here), a prominent Atlantic City attorney. He retained control of it for the next 60 years. (Courtesy of Jeanne Kirkman.)

Despite the Great Depression, Kirkman maintained a huge staff at the hotel. He continued to keep Locksley Hall for the male staff. Business continued to boom during these years, even as the Depression had its effects elsewhere.

Kirkman kept a full staff of cooks, maids, doormen, bellhops, and beach and pool workers throughout the years, and guests continued to fill the hotel to near capacity. The pools were especially popular, even with those not staying at the hotel.

When the property for the hotel was bought by the Ocean Front Hotel Corporation, automobiles were just becoming a popular mode of transportation. Seeing the future, the group bought 1.8 acres across Eleventh Street, directly opposite where the hotel was to be built, to be used as a parking lot. By the early 1930s, most guests were arriving at the hotel in automobiles.

On Friday, July 9, 1937, the third annual Atlantic Coast Swim Championship, sponsored by the Kiwanis Club, was held at the Flanders Hotel pools. The swim meet and carnival were held to benefit the Kiwanis Club's Underprivileged Children's Fund. Among those competing was Dorothy Forbes, "America's Back Stroke Queen," and Peter Fick, "World's 100-Meter Champion."

THIRD ANNUAL
ATLANTIC COAST
SWIM CHAMPIONSHIP

**KIWANIS**

# SWIM
# MEET

*and* CARNIVAL

Under Auspices of Middle Atlantic A. A. U.

# TONITE
*7:45 P. M.*

# FLANDERS'
# POOLS

Benefit—

**Kiwanis Underprivileged
Children's Fund**

On August 7, 1937, the formal dedication of Ocean City's new $100,000 post office building took place. The schedule was as follows: "12:30 p.m. dedication exercises in front of the new post office building at Ninth Street and Ocean Avenue; 1:15 p.m. aviation luncheon in Flanders Hotel; 3:30 p.m. airplane recreates the historic flight of August 5, 1912 when the first airmail flight in New Jersey took place, flying between Ocean City and Stone Harbor." Here, the Flanders Hotel's main dining room is set, awaiting the post office and aviation dignitaries.

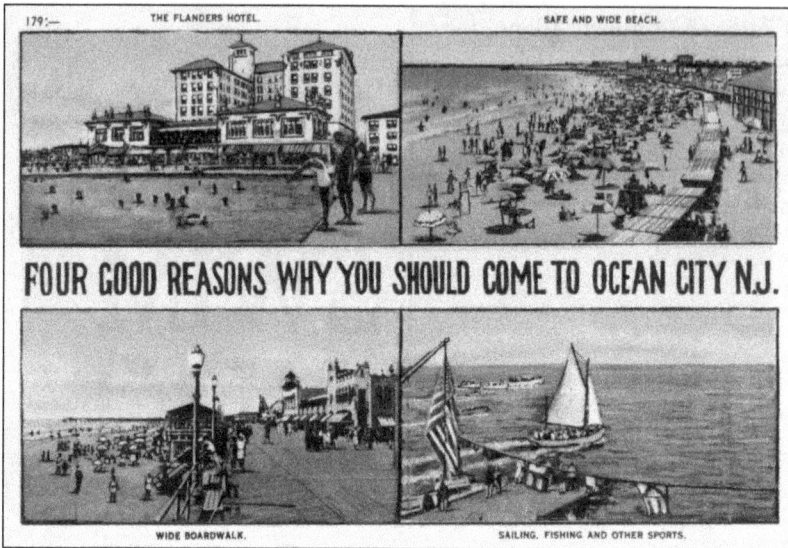

FOUR GOOD REASONS WHY YOU SHOULD COME TO OCEAN CITY N.J.

THE FLANDERS HOTEL.

SAFE AND WIDE BEACH.

WIDE BOARDWALK.

SAILING, FISHING AND OTHER SPORTS.

In this popular postcard from the 1930s, the Flanders Hotel (upper left) is one of the "Four Good Reasons Why You Should Come to Ocean City N.J."

In 1943, the Navy began using the Flanders swimming pools as training areas. Sailors from the Atlantic County Naval Training Station came, 75 at a time, to take a series of lessons. Every Tuesday and Thursday for most of the summer, the men were brought to the pools to get acclimated to swimming, diving, jumping, and rescue work in salt water. They were taught proper swimming technique, staying underwater, jumping and diving from the high board, rescue holds, and other water practices. (Courtesy of Barb and Dean Adams.)

Adjoining the hotel's swimming pools were tennis courts, a shuffleboard court, and a miniature-golf course. These, unlike the swimming pools, were open for hotel guests and their guests only. There were dressing rooms and lockers for both women and men, with hot and cold saltwater baths. Golf, horseback riding, yachting, and fishing excursions could be arranged by the hotel staff.

The Flanders was on the American plan, serving three meals each day to hotel guests. The dining room was also open to the public. Breakfast was served either in the main dining room or in one of the smaller, less public rooms. Lunch was served in the dining rooms or around the pool, wherever the hotel's guests preferred. Dinner was always served in the main dining room, and guests were expected to dress for dinner—no casual clothes allowed!

During the 1940s, a string ensemble played in the grand lobby on the second floor, daily except Mondays. Special concerts were held there on Tuesday and Sunday evenings. During the 1930s, this room was referred to as the "Exchange." (Courtesy of Barb and Dean Adams.)

In this view of the formal second-floor lobby, the top of the curving marble staircase leading up from the ground floor lobby can be seen. Guests could be brought upstairs by one of two elevators. A grand piano, often played by the guests at their leisure or by professionals for affairs, was always kept in tune. The formal dining rooms and ballrooms were on this floor, as were a ladies' and a men's cloakroom.

The ground-floor lobby was less formal than the upstairs main lobby. Guests could lounge there with friends, read the newspaper, and relax. The stairs in this photograph lead up to the shopping lane, where select stores displayed their wares.

Soon after the Flanders Hotel opened, stories began circulating that a woman in a long, flowing white gown was seen wandering the hotel. Her identity is a mystery, but she is called Emily. She is said by hotel employees to be mischievous rather than destructive, and she has been heard singing in the hallways. Artist Tony Troy painted her picture on a wall in a second-floor corridor of the hotel, using descriptions by those who profess to have seen her.

The Flanders Hotel staff set up a private Cabana Colony and Cabana Casino, which served late breakfasts and luncheons daily from late June to early September. The Colony was available for hotel guests and their friends. Grace Kelly and her older sister Margaret frequently enjoyed the facility, especially when their brother Jack was a lifeguard on the beach in front of the hotel.

The 1950 Miss New Jersey Pageant, sponsored by the Exchange Club of Ocean City, was held on Saturday, July 8, at the Flanders Hotel pools. Seating for 3,000 spectators was arranged around the pools. This was the first time the pageant was held in Ocean City; it had been held in Asbury Park in previous years. June Stephens of Ship Bottom, Ocean County, was named Miss New Jersey. She participated in the Miss America Pageant held later that summer in Atlantic City.

# Four

# FLANDERS HOTEL AND LIFEGUARDS— PERFECT TOGETHER

Although the Flanders Hotel was doing well financially and was a place local people looked to for special events, general manager J. Howard Slocum wanted to make the hotel a more regional attraction. In 1924, when a small, guests-only swimming pool was opened, he asked Jack Jernee, captain of the Ocean City Beach Patrol, to have his lifeguards give swimming and diving exhibitions at the pool to entertain the hotel's guests. In return, Slocum would give permission for the lifeguards to use the pool before and after their work hours to practice their skills. Jernee agreed, and this was the beginning of a long relationship between the beach patrol and the Flanders Hotel.

After the fire of 1927, when the city rebuilt the boardwalk a half-block closer to the ocean, there was a large empty area between the hotel and the ocean. To remedy this, Slocum suggested filling the space with a large swimming pool. In July 1929, three new saltwater pools opened in the space. The main pool was Olympic-sized, another was a shallow children's pool, and one was a deeper, diving pool. With the opening of the new pools, the era of the giant water carnivals directed by Jernee and performed by the beach patrol at the Flanders' pools began. The water shows were so successful and popular that Slocum had the main pool area lined with bleachers to accommodate the crowds.

The 1934 National Lifeguard Tournament was held on the Tenth Street beach, and the beach patrol hosted a formal ball and buffet supper in the Flanders Hotel ballroom later that evening. Many distinguished guests attended, including Pres. Franklin Roosevelt's son and daughter-in-law and the commander of the US Coast Guard, Rear Adm. H.G. Hamlet. From 1929 to 1937, the South Jersey Lifeguard Swim Meet was held in the Flanders' pool. The Atlantic Coast Relay Races were held there as well. In 1939, the lifeguards held their first reunion in the Flanders ballroom. They were celebrating Jernee's 20th year as captain of the beach patrol.

In this image, the Ocean City Beach Patrol (OCBP) headquarters can be seen at center, on the beach at Tenth Street. The headquarters was literally in the shadow cast by the Flanders Hotel. The proximity of the two helped forge the relationship between the lifeguards and the hotel.

Each year, the lifeguards took a group photograph, and it was always taken on the beach with the Flanders Hotel in the background. The 1925 beach patrol squad is seen here. The men in white at far right are, from left to right, beach patrol medic Dudley Cone, Dr. Wettherill B. Ellison, Dr. C. Eugene Darby, and beach patrol captain Jack Jernee. The young mascot in front is Russell Leary, who later became a member of the patrol.

The swimming pool at the Flanders Hotel opened on May 30, 1924. Located between the hotel's solariums, the pool was the site of weekly aquatic shows, put on by members of the Ocean City Beach Patrol. The final show of the first season was held on August 23. Spectators were there to watch the beach patrol's intrasquad races. There were five swimming races, a diving contest, and a canoe-tilting contest. The announcer was W. Ward Beam, who led calisthenics classes on the beach each morning. He is seen at lower left with his famous megaphone.

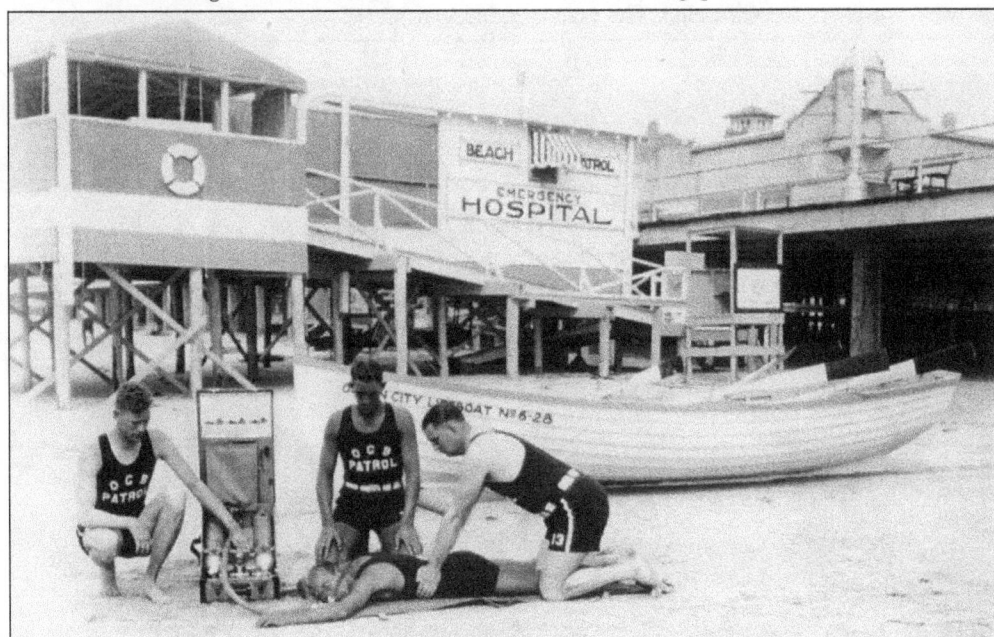

Beach patrol captain Jack Jernee brought the American Red Cross to the Flanders Hotel in August 1925. They were there to stage an exhibition to show the audience how to break the grip of a drowning person and how to best resuscitate a drowning victim. The exhibition aimed to stop venturesome swimmers from taking undue risks. Over 500 people witnessed the event. In this photograph, lifeguards are practicing the techniques exhibited by the Red Cross volunteers.

The swimming pool at the Flanders Hotel was the setting for a water polo match in the summer of 1925, as seen in this photograph. The match pitted Ocean City lifeguards from the northern stands against those from the southern stands. The game, refereed by Ewing T. Corson, was fast and furious and provided many thrills for the spectators. Due to Corson's efforts, several clashes between the teams were avoided. The match ended in a 3-3 tie.

Posing here are, from left to right, beach patrol captain Jack Jernee, Lockwood Miller, Lee Johnson, beach patrol lieutenant Charles Schock, Lloyd Sheppard, and Cook Marshall. Sheppard and Marshall were the 1925 two-man rescue boat champions. These men organized the water shows at the Flanders pool.

116

The lifeguards used the Flanders Hotel swimming pool before and after work to improve their lifesaving skills and practice for their water shows. Here, Frank McKee practices one of his dives for the water show. On August 20, 1926, the guards demonstrated their speed by winning the South Jersey Lifeguard Swim Meet.

**TODAY**

Formal Opening

OF THE

**NEW FLANDERS POOLS**

Water Sports                    Aquatic Exhibition

—Music By—

CAPE MAY COUNTY AMERICAN LEGION BAND

—Life Saving Exhibition by—

OCEAN CITY BEACH PATROL

SMITH BROS.              JAMES McCLURE

COMEDIANS OF THE SEA         THE HUMAN FISH

FUN -- FARCE -- SKILL      See him swim the length of the
                          pool, 150 feet, under water.

BALLOON RACE                NOVELTY EVENTS

**Admission Free to Spectators**

BATHING IN POOL, 50c        BATH HOUSE, 75c
                          (including pool privileges)

Pool Open from 9 A. M. until 10 P. M.

Special Arrangements Can Be Made For Exclusive Use of Pool By Evening Bathing Parties

Kiddies' Wading Pool          Deep Pool          Guard Protection

Swimming Instructions for Adults and Children

**ERNIE WIESE, Mgr.**

This is an advertisement for the formal opening of the new pools. A lifesaving exhibition put on by the OCBP was a feature of the event. This poster was put up all over the city. The event took place on July 27, 1929. Admission was free for spectators.

With the opening of the new pools, the era of the Ocean City Beach Patrol's giant water shows began. As this photograph shows, the bleachers surrounding the largest pool were always filled with people, there to watch the exciting spectaculars designed by beach patrol captain Jernee.

Captain Jernee scored a coup when he was able to get Olympic champion Johnny Weissmuller to participate in one of the Flanders water shows. On August 23, 1929, Weissmuller competed there against the beach patrol's best swimmers. Weissmuller, who held most of the Olympic sprint records, won the event with a time of 55 seconds in the 100-yard freestyle.

# WATER SPORTS CARNIVAL
## Friday Evening, August 23

FEATURING

### JOHNNY WEISMULLER
AND
### HAROLD "STUBBY" KREUGER
NATIONAL AQUATIC STARS

## Flanders Hotel Pools
11th and Boardwalk

Jernee also managed to get Harold "Stubby" Kreuger, the 1924 Olympic backstroke champion and "Comedy King," to perform in the August 23 show. Kreuger swam the backstroke in one minute, nine seconds, the best time seen in the Flanders pool. Weissmuller and Kreuger teamed up for a comedy act in the pool that was well received by the 5,000 spectators surrounding the pool.

The 1930 Ocean City Beach Patrol swim team trained at the Flanders pool before reporting for work. Shown here are, from left to right, Capt. Jack Jernee, Pep Smith, Frank McKee, Marley Fitzgerald, Ed Kelly, Ed Bardo, Frank Holt, Bill Brown, Fran Hoffman, Robert Beatty, Bill Ennis, Bill Briggs, and John Gooley.

Vice Pres. Charles Curtis was greeted by Ocean City officials when he arrived at the Flanders Hotel on July 3, 1930. He was in town to celebrate the Fourth of July and the 50th anniversary of the Tabernacle Association. Curtis wanted to see Ocean City's famous beach and boardwalk, so Mayor Joseph G. Champion took him to the Tenth Street OCBP headquarters, where he met Captain Jernee. They climbed to the top of the building, where they had an excellent view of the boardwalk, beach, Atlantic Ocean, and Flanders Hotel.

-- PROGRAM --

# NATIONAL LIFE GUARD

# TOURNAMENT

Held Under the Auspices of the

## City of Ocean City

...at...

## Ocean City, New Jersey

# July 26th, 1934

*Trophies to be Awarded*

NATIONAL TEAM CHAMPIONSHIP
Presented by the City of Ocean City, N. J.

NATIONAL INDIVIDUAL CHAMPIONSHIP
Presented by the City of Ocean City, N. J.

*Price 25c*

The 1934 National Lifeguard Tournament races were held on July 26 on the Tenth Street beach. Lifeguard Englebert Loeper is pictured on the cover of the tournament book. The festivities after the races included a lifeguard water circus in the Flanders pool and a formal ball in the Flanders ballroom. Distinguished visitors attending the affair included Mr. and Mrs. James Roosevelt, son and daughter-in-law of the president; the Honorable Ernest Lee Jahncke, former assistant secretary of the Navy under President Hoover; and commander of the US Coast Guard, Rear Adm. H.G. Hamlet. Tickets cost $2.50 each and entitled one to all of the Flanders events, including the buffet supper at 11:00 p.m.

The Ocean City Beach Patrol won the 1934 National Lifeguard Tournament. In this photograph, Mayor Harry Headley (left) presents the winning trophy to Bob Stretch (second from left) and Bert Loeper, while Capt. Jack Jernee (far right) looks on.

On July 15, 1938, in the Flanders Hotel swimming pool, the Ocean City Beach Patrol won the Atlantic Coast Relay Championship for the third straight year. The guards were cheered on by 3,000 spectators. In this photograph, Captain Jernee poses with the relay team. Shown are, from left to right, Bob Monihan, Reggie Kaithern, Jernee, Ed Kelly, and Ed Gilbert.

The July 27, 1939, *Sentinel-Ledger* has the headlines "Lifeguard Beauties to Strut at Pool" and "Two-Score Gallivantin' Greek Gods on Parade Tomorrow Nite at Flanders." The article goes on to describe how the Ocean City Beach Patrol Benevolent Organization decided to parody the Miss America pageant. All of the members of the beach patrol were to participate as part of the water show to be held at the Flanders Hotel pools the next evening. The judges would be women from the yacht club. The guards in this photograph are, from left to right, Russell Leary, Lewis Carey, Paul Roselle, and George Lafferty. The following were banned from the competition: "1. Winking at the judges. 2. More than a six-inch hip sway. 3. Page-boy bobs. 4. Fan dances. 5. Two-piece suits with space in between."

On August 26, 1939, the first lifeguard reunion was held at the Flanders Hotel. It commemorated Jack Jernee's 20th year as captain of the Ocean City Beach Patrol. In this group photograph of the 1939 beach patrol, those in the first row are, from left to right, beach medic Emerson Burkhardt, Capt. Jernee, Mayor George D. Richards, beach patrol doctor C. Eugene Darby, and beach medic Joseph John. The public was invited to both a water show at the Flanders pool on Friday evening and the reunion party on Saturday evening. All of these men, and others, celebrated at the reunion.

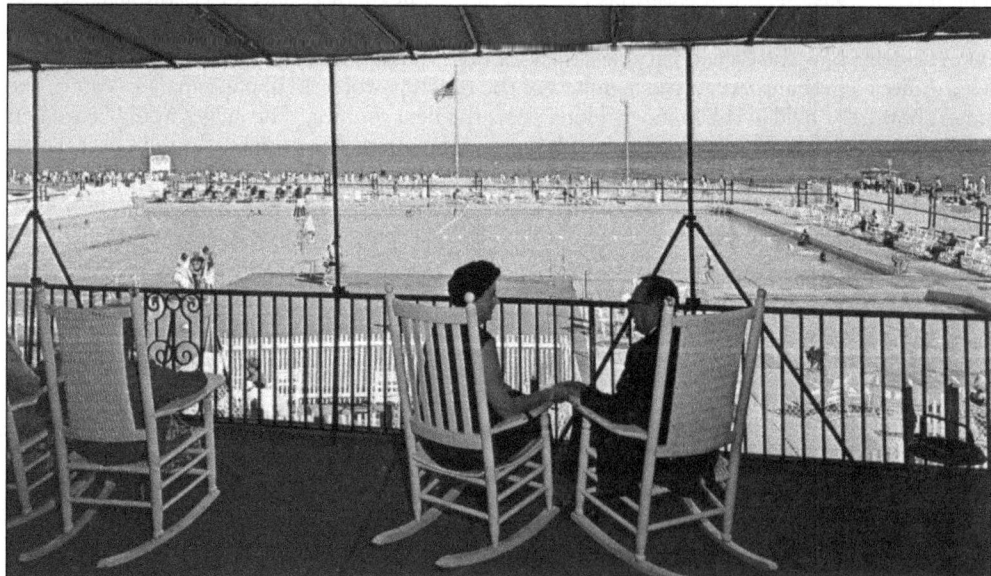

From this covered porch at the Flanders Hotel, guests had a perfect view of the large pool. From there, they could see the water spectaculars put on by the lifeguards or just enjoy the view of swimmers at the pool and of the beach and ocean beyond.

124

# *Diamond Jubilee*
# WATER SHOW

### FLANDERS POOL

8:30 P. M.

### SATURDAY, AUGUST 14th, 1954

*SPONSORED BY*

## OCEAN CITY EXCHANGE CLUB

Benefit of Scholarship Fund

In 1954, Ocean City held a yearlong diamond jubilee to celebrate 75 years since the city's founding. One of the most highly attended events was the Diamond Jubilee Water Show, held at the Flanders Hotel Pool on August 14. For the program, sponsored by the Ocean City Exchange Club as a benefit for its scholarship fund, a capacity crowd of 2,500 positioned themselves around the three pools to watch the water spectacle. The eight-event program showcasing lifeguards' skills was designed by the former captain of the beach patrol, Jack G. Jernee, who had developed the water shows held at the Flanders pools starting in the 1920s.

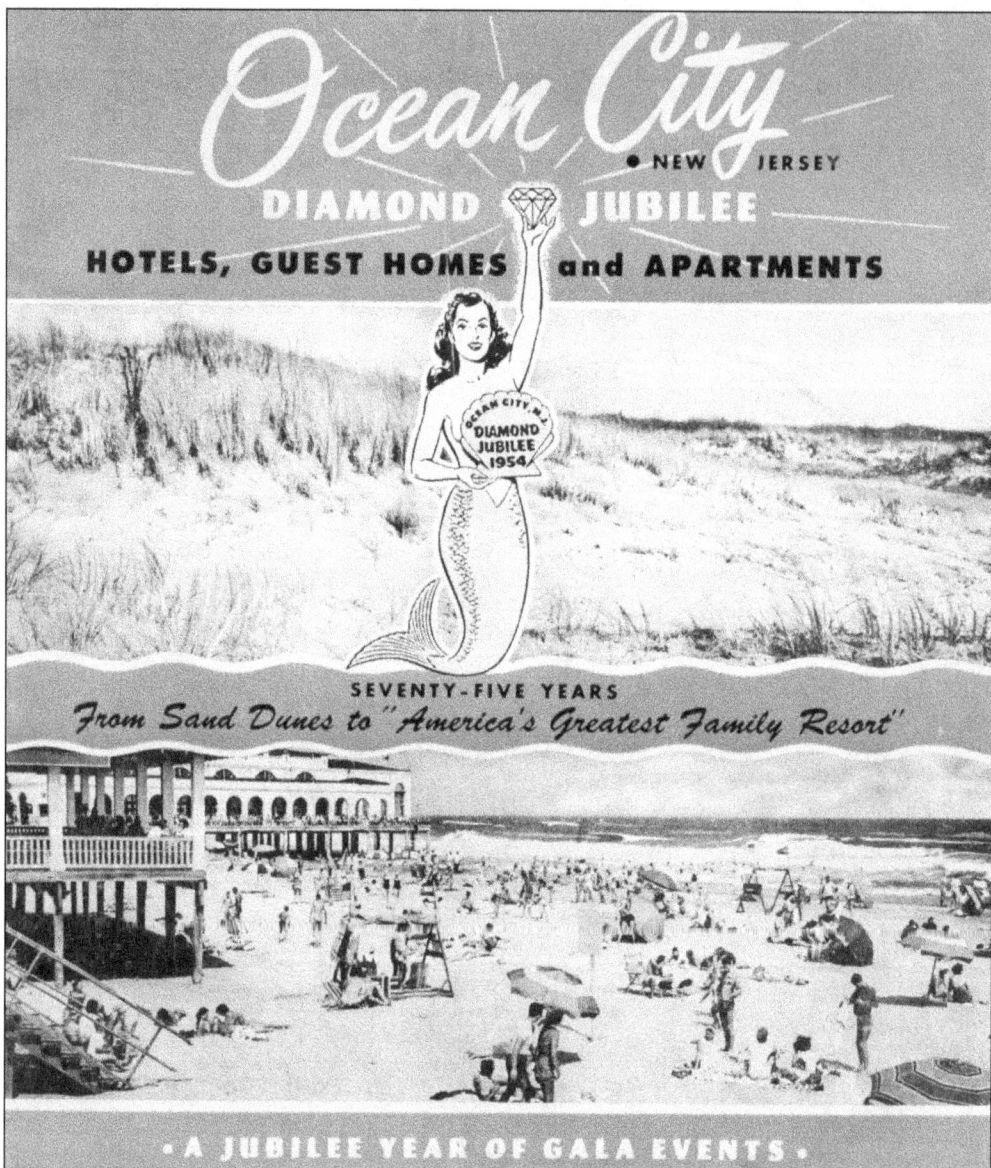

The *Hotels, Guest Homes, and Apartments* directory was published each year to give the "traveling public an informative booklet that will help in planning a vacation in Ocean City." Every year, the Flanders Hotel and the safety of the city's beaches were prominently advertised. The diamond jubilee of Ocean City, held in 1954, celebrated 75 years since the city's founding. The motto for the year was "From Sand Dunes to America's Greatest Family Resort." Shown here is the cover of the 1954 directory.

# INDEX

Visit us at
arcadiapublishing.com

· · · · · · · · · · · · · · · · · · · · · · · · · · · · · · · · · · · · · · · · · · · · · · · · ·

www.ingramcontent.com/pod-product-compliance
Lightning Source LLC
Chambersburg PA
CBHW050709110426
42813CB00007B/2135